United States Government Accountability Office

Report to the Ranking Member, Subcommittee on Oversight, Committee on Science, Space, and Technology, House of Representatives

September 2013

I0448430

MANAGING CRITICAL ISOTOPES

Stewardship of Lithium-7 Is Needed to Ensure a Stable Supply

GAO Highlights

Highlights of GAO-13-716, a report to the Ranking Member, Subcommittee on Oversight, Committee on Science, Space, and Technology, House of Representatives

MANAGING CRITICAL ISOTOPES

Stewardship of Lithium-7 Is Needed to Ensure a Stable Supply

Why GAO Did This Study

About 13 percent of our nation's electricity is produced by pressurized water reactors that rely on lithium-7, an isotope of lithium produced and exported solely by China and Russia, for their safe operation. Lithium-7 is added to the water that cools the reactor core to prevent the cooling water from becoming acidic. Without the lithium-7, the cooling water's acidity would increase the rate of corrosion of pipes and other infrastructure—possibly causing them to fail. Utilities that operate the pressurized water reactors have experienced little difficulty obtaining lithium-7, but they may not be aware of all the risks of relying on two producers.

GAO was asked to review the supply and domestic demand for lithium-7 and how risks are being managed. This report examines (1) what is known about the supply and demand of lithium-7, (2) what federal agencies are responsible for managing supply risks, and (3) alternative options to mitigate a potential shortage. GAO reviewed documents and interviewed officials from DOE, NNSA, and NRC, in addition to industry representatives. This report is an unclassified version of a classified report also issued in September 2013.

What GAO Recommends

GAO recommends that the Secretary of Energy ensure a stable future supply of lithium-7 by directing the Isotope Program to take on a stewardship role for lithium-7 by taking steps, including fully assessing risks and accurately determining domestic demand. DOE concurred with the recommendation.

View GAO-13-716. For more information, contact David C. Trimble, (202) 512-3841 or trimbled@gao.gov or Dr. Timothy M. Persons, (202) 512-6412 or personst@gao.gov.

What GAO Found

Little is known about lithium-7 production in China and Russia and whether their supplies can meet future domestic demand. According to industry representatives, China and Russia produce enough lithium-7 to meet demand from U.S. pressurized water reactors, a type of commercial nuclear power reactor that requires lithium-7 for safe operation. However, China's continued supply may be reduced by its own growing demand, according to an expert that is familiar with China's plans. Specifically, China is building several pressurized water reactors and developing a new type of reactor that will require 1,000s of kilograms of lithium-7 to operate, rather than the 300 kilograms needed annually for all 65 U.S. pressurized water reactors. Relying on two producers of lithium-7 leaves U.S. pressurized water reactors vulnerable to lithium-7 supply disruptions.

No federal entity has taken stewardship responsibility for assessing and managing risks to the lithium-7 supply, but DOE is taking some steps. Risk assessment is the identification and analysis of relevant risks, communication of risks to stakeholders, and then taking steps to manage the risks, according to federal standards for internal control. Officials at DOE, the National Nuclear Security Administration (NNSA), and the Nuclear Regulatory Commission (NRC) told GAO they view lithium-7 as a commercial commodity for which industry is responsible. Industry representatives told GAO that they had no concerns about the lithium-7 supply, as they have experienced no problems in obtaining it. But GAO learned that industry representatives may not be familiar with all the supply risks. Notwithstanding, DOE plans to set aside 200 kilograms of lithium-7 and is funding research on lithium-7 production methods. DOE also studied lithium-7 supply and demand and concluded that no further action is needed. However, GAO found several shortcomings in its study, including that DOE underestimated the amount of lithium-7 used domestically. Industry estimates show that about 300 kilograms of lithium-7 are used annually in the United States, whereas DOE estimated that 200 kilograms are used annually. This and other shortcomings make it unclear if DOE's conclusion is correct that no additional action is needed.

Based on information from agency officials and industry representatives, GAO identified three options to mitigate a potential lithium-7 shortage: (1) building a domestic reserve is a low-cost option that could help in the short-term; (2) building a domestic production capability is a longer-term solution that could eliminate lithium-7 imports, but take about 5 years and cost $10-12 million, according to NNSA; and (3) reducing pressurized water reactors' reliance on lithium-7 is another longer-term solution, but may require years of research and changes in how reactors are operated.

Contents

Abbreviations

EPRI	Electric Power Research Institute
Isotope Program	Isotope Development and Production for Research and Applications program
NNSA	National Nuclear Security Administration
NRC	Nuclear Regulatory Commission
Y-12	Y-12 National Security Complex

September 19, 2013

The Honorable Dan Maffei
Ranking Member
Subcommittee on Oversight
Committee on Science, Space, and Technology
House of Representatives

Dear Mr. Maffei:

About 13 percent of our nation's electricity is produced by 65 nuclear power reactors that rely on enriched lithium hydroxide—a chemical that is produced and exported only by China and Russia. Of the 100 commercial nuclear power reactors in the United States, these 65 are pressurized water reactors, a type of reactor that requires lithium hydroxide to be added to the water that cools it. The lithium hydroxide is used in pressurized water reactors to prevent the cooling water from becoming acidic due to the addition of other chemicals that are critical to managing the nuclear reaction. Without the lithium hydroxide, the cooling water's acidity would increase the rate of corrosion of pipes and other infrastructure in the reactor—possibly causing them to fail. Lithium hydroxide is made using lithium-7, an isotope of lithium that does not interfere with the nuclear reaction within a reactor core.[1] Lithium-7 is also used in special purifiers called demineralizers that extract radioactive material and contaminants from the cooling water.[2] Low enriched lithium-7 was produced in the United States by the Y-12 National Security Complex (Y-12) in Oak Ridge, Tennessee, from 1955 to 1963 as a by-product of producing lithium-6, which is used in the nuclear weapons program. DOE has not needed to produce additional lithium-6 since that time and, according to Y-12 officials, the department sold the resulting supply of low-enriched lithium-7 on the open market, except for a limited

---

[1] Isotopes are varieties of a given chemical element with the same number of protons but different numbers of neutrons. For example, the helium-3 isotope, which is used in research and to detect neutrons in radiation detection equipment, has one less neutron than the helium-4 isotope, which is the helium isotope commonly used in party balloons.

[2] For the purposes of this report, we use the term lithium-7 when we describe the supply and demand for lithium-7 and/or lithium hydroxide that is made with lithium-7. Additionally, all quantities are expressed in terms of the weight of lithium-7 and not the weight of the lithium hydroxide that it is found in.

quantity.[3] Today, industry relies on China and Russia for its supply of lithium-7. According to industry representatives, utilities that operate pressurized water reactors have experienced little to no problems obtaining lithium-7 when they have needed it.

Lithium-7 has not been produced in the United States since 1963, but a portion of the low-enriched lithium-7 was further enriched and is stored by the National Nuclear Security Administration (NNSA),[4] a semiautonomous agency within DOE. Specifically, about 1,300 kilograms of lithium-7 (about 2,860 pounds), in the form of lithium hydroxide, was enriched to 99.99 percent—the level needed for use in pressurized water reactors—and stored at Y-12. However, according to Y-12 documentation, this supply has become contaminated during storage and would need to be purified before it is usable in a pressurized water reactor.[5] NNSA makes this supply available to DOE's Isotope Development and Production for Research and Applications program (Isotope Program) to sell for research and other purposes.[6] Similarly, NNSA makes other isotopes available to the Isotope Program to sell, including helium-3, on which we previously reported.[7] According to DOE, the Isotope Program's three-pronged mission is to: (1) produce or distribute isotopes in short supply, their associated by-products and surplus materials, and deliver isotope-related services; (2) maintain the infrastructure required to produce and supply isotopes and related services; and (3) investigate and develop

---

[3]The by-product of producing lithium-6 was slightly enriched lithium-7, according to DOE, which was sold on the open market. Y-12 later enriched some of the low-enriched lithium-7 to a level that could be used in pressurized water reactors.

[4]Congress created NNSA as a semiautonomous agency within DOE. NNSA is responsible for the management and security of the nation's nuclear weapons, nonproliferation, and naval reactors programs.

[5]In addition to the approximately 1,300 kilograms of lithium hydroxide, NNSA has about 400 kilograms of lithium-7 (about 882 pounds) that is enriched to 99.99 percent lithium-7, but is in a different chemical form and would need to be purified and converted to lithium hydroxide before it can be used in a pressurized water reactor. Approximately 8,600 kilograms of lithium-7 (about 18,900 pounds) are not enriched to 99.99 percent lithium-7, making it unusable in a pressurized water reactor.

[6]The Isotope Program provides over 300 different isotopes for sale, including lithium-7, for commercial and research applications.

[7]GAO, *Managing Critical Isotopes: Weaknesses in DOE's Management of Helium-3 Delayed the Federal Response to a Critical Supply Shortage*, GAO-11-472 (Washington, D.C.: May 12, 2011).

new or improved isotope production and processing techniques that can make new isotopes available for research and other applications.

The 65 pressurized water reactors that rely on lithium hydroxide are owned and operated by utility companies and provide electricity to the electrical grid. For the purposes of this report, these utilities, as well as trade organizations, such as the Electric Power Research Institute (EPRI),[8] make up the nuclear power industry that relies on lithium-7. All commercial nuclear power reactors in the United States, including the 65 pressurized water reactors, are regulated by the Nuclear Regulatory Commission (NRC) through licensing, inspection, and enforcement of its requirements. NRC's regulations govern certain aspects of the cooling water, according to NRC officials, but not the specific chemicals used in the cooling water, including lithium-7. Utilities that operate pressurized water reactors purchase their lithium hydroxide from lithium-7 brokers. According to industry representatives and lithium-7 brokers, there are three brokers that purchase lithium hydroxide directly from China or Russia and then sell it to U.S. companies for use in pressurized water reactors and in the manufacture of demineralizers. While some utilities and demineralizer manufacturers may purchase lithium-hydroxide directly from China or Russia, according to a lithium-7 broker, most lithium hydroxide used in the United States is purchased through the three brokers.

In light of the risk of relying on two suppliers for a critical component used in most of the nation's commercial nuclear power reactors, you asked us to review lithium-7 supply and demand in the United States. This report examines (1) what is known about the supply and domestic demand for lithium-7; (2) the responsibilities of DOE, NRC, and other entities in assessing risks to the lithium-7 supply, and what, if anything, has been done to mitigate a potential supply disruption of lithium-7; and (3) additional options, if any, identified by government officials and industry representatives for mitigating a potential lithium-7 shortage. In September 2013, we reported to you on the results of our work in a classified report; this is an unclassified version of that report.

---

[8]The Electric Power Research Institute conducts research, development, and demonstration relating to the generation, delivery, and use of electricity for the benefit of the public. Its work spans nearly every area of electricity generation, including commercial nuclear power.

Scope and Methodology

To determine what is known about the supply and domestic demand for lithium-7, we analyzed data provided by industry representatives, reviewed agency and industry documents, and interviewed agency officials and industry representatives. Specifically, to understand the supply and domestic demand of lithium-7, we reviewed data from the three brokers that purchase lithium hydroxide from China and Russia and sell it to utilities and other companies in the United States. To assess the reliability of the data, we interviewed lithium-7 brokers about the data and found the data to be sufficiently reliable for purposes of this report. We also obtained information on China's supply and demand for lithium-7 from an expert on nuclear reactors at the Massachusetts Institute of Technology that was identified by DOE and Y-12 officials. Additionally, this expert has been working with DOE in its meetings with scientists from the Chinese Academy of Sciences regarding China's research on new reactor designs. We also reviewed documents provided by DOE, Y-12, and two utilities that operate pressurized water reactors—Tennessee Valley Authority (TVA) and Exelon. We also interviewed representatives of companies that buy, sell, and/or handle lithium hydroxide, including Ceradyne, Inc., Isoflex, Nukem Isotopes, and Sigma Aldrich and officials from DOE, NNSA, and Y-12.

To examine the responsibilities of DOE, NRC, and other entities in assessing risks to the lithium-7 supply, and what, if anything, has been done to mitigate a potential supply disruption of lithium-7, we reviewed documents from DOE, Y-12, and NRC. We also interviewed officials from DOE's Isotope Program and the Office of Nuclear Energy; NNSA's Office of Nuclear Materials Integration, Office of Nuclear Nonproliferation and International Security, and Y-12; and NRC. We also interviewed representatives from Exelon, TVA, EPRI, North American Electric Reliability Corporation, Nuclear Energy Institute, Pressurized Water Reactors Owners Group, Ceradyne, Inc., and Isoflex. In addition, we compared actions DOE is taking to manage and communicate lithium-7 supply risks with federal standards for internal control.[9]

To identify additional options, if any, for mitigating a potential lithium-7 shortage, we reviewed technical articles and documents from industry and academia, DOE, Y-12, and NRC. We also interviewed officials from

---

[9]GAO, *Standards for Internal Control in the Federal Government*, GAO/AIMD-00-21.3.1 ("Green Book") (Washington, D.C.: November 1999).

DOE's Isotope Program, Office of Nuclear Energy, and Idaho National Laboratory; Y-12; and representatives from Exelon, TVA, and EPRI.

We conducted this performance audit from June 2012 to September 2013 in accordance with generally accepted government auditing standards. Those standards require that we plan and perform the audit to obtain sufficient, appropriate evidence to provide a reasonable basis for our findings and conclusions based on our audit objectives. We believe that the evidence obtained provides a reasonable basis for our findings and conclusions based on our audit objectives.

Background

Lithium-7 was produced in the United States as a by-product of enriching lithium-6 for the United States' nuclear weapons program. Lithium-7 and lithium-6 are derived from natural lithium, which contains about 92.5 percent lithium-7 and about 7.5 percent lithium-6. Lithium-6 was enriched in the United States by separating it from lithium-7 using a column exchange process, called COLEX, that required very large quantities of mercury, which can harm human health and the environment. Y-12 built a COLEX facility and began operations in 1955 and used it through 1963 to enrich lithium-6 and lithium-7.[10] Y-12 experienced several problems with the COLEX process, including equipment failures, worker exposure to mercury, and mercury contamination of the environment. Y-12 shut the COLEX facility down in 1963 and has not operated it since then. While the United States still has a stockpile of lithium-6, DOE sold the lithium-7 by-product to commercial companies, though some was enriched and still remains stored at Y-12.

Lithium-7 is used in two functions of a pressurized water reactor—to produce lithium hydroxide that is added to the cooling water to reduce the acidity, and lithium-7 is added to demineralizers to filter contaminants out of the cooling water. The cooling water becomes acidic due to the addition of boric acid, which contains boron-10, an isotope of boron that is used to manage the nuclear reaction in the core—the use of both boron-10 and lithium hydroxide is based on reactor core design requirements and water pH requirements for corrosion control. Lithium hydroxide, made with lithium-7 rather than lithium-6, is added to the cooling water to

---

[10]The COLEX process separated the two lithium isotopes by using natural lithium dissolved in mercury and other chemicals. Lithium-6 is more attracted to the mercury than lithium-7, which is more attracted to the other chemicals, thus separating the two isotopes.

reduce the acidity of the water and boric acid. Lithium-7 is used rather than lithium-6 or natural lithium, which contains lithium-6, because lithium-6 would react with nuclear material in the reactor core to produce tritium, a radioactive isotope of hydrogen. According to industry representatives, lithium hydroxide is added directly to the cooling water, via a chemical feed tank, when a pressurized water reactor is started up after being shut down, such as after refueling. Lithium-7 is also used in special water purifiers—called demineralizers—that remove radioactive material and impurities from the cooling water. Figure 1 shows the flow of water through a typical pressurized water reactor, though some variations among reactors may exist. As the cooling water circulates in the primary cooling loop, as shown in figure 1, some of the water flows through pipes to the demineralizers and the chemical feed tank where the lithium hydroxide is added.

GAO-13-716 Managing Critical Isotopes

Figure 1: Pressurized Water Reactor Showing Where Lithium-7 is Incorporated Into the Cooling Water

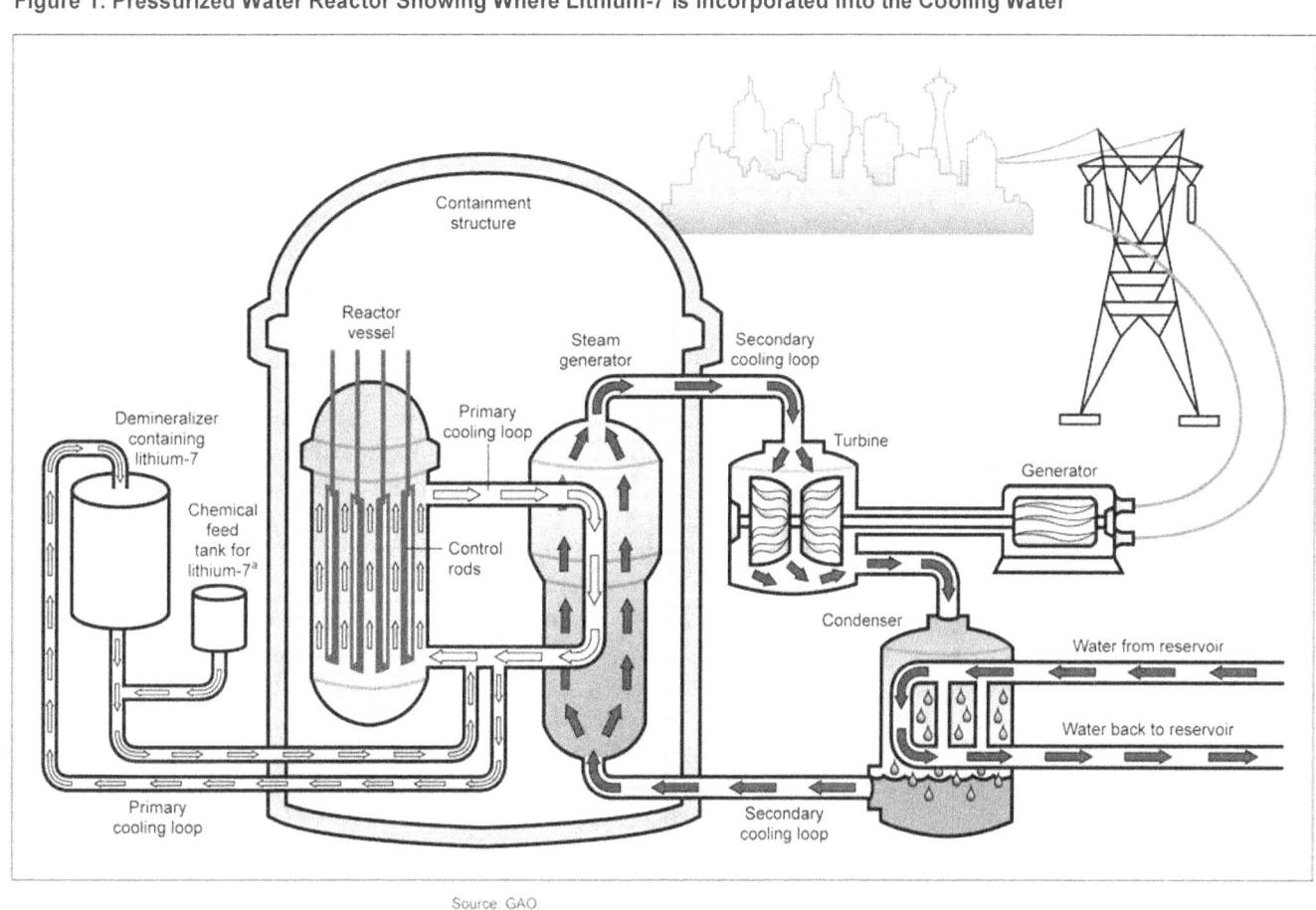

Source: GAO

[a]Lithium-7, in the form of lithium hydroxide, is added to the cooling water using the chemical feed tank.

Little Is Known about Lithium-7 Production, Creating Uncertainty about the Reliability of the Future Supply

There is no domestic production of lithium-7, and little is known about the lithium-7 production capabilities of China and Russia and whether they will be able to provide future supplies. China and Russia produce lithium-7 as a by-product of enriching lithium-6 for their nuclear weapons programs, according to a DOE official, much like the United States previously did. Because of the secrecy of their weapons programs, China and Russia's lithium-7 production capabilities are not fully known, according to lithium-7 brokers. According to industry representatives, lithium-7 brokers, and NNSA documents, China and Russia have produced enough lithium-7 to meet the current U.S. demand, which is not expected to increase a significant amount in the near future, based on

DOE's information that shows five new pressurized water reactors scheduled to begin operating by 2018. Additionally, during the course of our review, utilities announced that four pressurized water reactors would be decommissioned, eliminating their demand for lithium-7.

China's continued supply of lithium-7 may be reduced by its own growing demand created by the construction of new reactors and the development of new reactor designs. China's demand is expected to increase because, according to information from DOE, the International Atomic Energy Agency,[11] and an expert on nuclear reactors who has met with Chinese scientists on this topic, China is constructing over 25 pressurized water reactors that are scheduled to begin operating by 2015. Additionally, China is planning to build a new type of nuclear power reactor—a molten salt reactor—that will require dramatically larger amounts of lithium-7 to operate.[12] China is pursuing the development of two different types of molten salt reactors, according to the expert, each of which will result in a reactor that requires 1,000s of kilograms of lithium-7 to operate, rather than the approximate 300 kilograms (about 660 pounds) annually needed for all 65 U.S. pressurized water reactors combined, according to lithium-7 brokers. China's first molten salt reactor is expected to be finished by 2017, and the second reactor by 2020, according to the reactor expert.[13] Furthermore, molten salt reactors require a more pure form of lithium-7—99.995 percent, or higher—than what is currently produced by China and Russia, according to the reactor expert and a lithium-7 broker. To obtain the higher enriched lithium-7, according to the reactor expert who is familiar with China's research, China built a small facility that will feed in lower-enriched lithium-7 and enrich it to the higher level of purity that is needed. An Isotope Program official suggested to us that China's new

---

[11]The International Atomic Energy Agency is an autonomous international organization affiliated with the United Nations, established in Vienna, Austria, in 1957. The agency has the dual role of promoting the peaceful uses of nuclear energy by transferring nuclear science and technology through its nuclear science and applications and technical cooperation programs and verifying, through its safeguards program, that nuclear material subject to safeguards is not diverted to nuclear weapons or other proscribed purposes.

[12]Molten salt reactors, unlke pressurized water reactors, do not use water to cool the reactor core; instead, a type of salt is liquefied and circulated through the core. The molten salt consists of lithium-7, in addition to other chemicals.

[13]According to the expert, China's first reactor, a fluoride salt-cooled, high-temperature reactor, referred to as an FHR, is being built first, followed by the molten salt reactor; both reactor designs use 1,000s of kilograms of lithium-7.

facility could increase the available supply of lithium-7 for pressurized water reactors. However, according to the reactor expert, this new facility may reduce the supply of lithium-7 available for export since it uses lithium-7 as feedstock. This expert said that China has obtained lithium-7 from its own supplies and has purchased additional lithium-7 from Russia to enrich in its own facility, possibly making China a net importer of lithium-7. It is unknown, however, whether China has enough lithium-7 for its increased nuclear fleet and molten salt reactors, or if it will need to import additional quantities, which could reduce the available supply of lithium-7. For example, one lithium-7 broker told us in June of this year that China had no lithium-7 that it could sell to this broker.

Russia's supply of lithium-7, on the other hand, may be largely available for export because Russia is believed to have very little domestic demand for lithium-7. Russia's fleet of pressurized water reactors does not use lithium hydroxide because they were specifically designed to use potassium hydroxide to lower the cooling water's acidity. However, because Russia's production capacity of lithium-7 is not known, U.S. utilities cannot be assured that Russia will continue to meet their demand for lithium-7 as China's demand increases. For example, one lithium-7 broker told us in June 2013 that he is having difficulty getting lithium-7 from Russia, though he is unsure if it is because Russia is unable to meet demand or for some other reason.

The risk of relying on so few producers of lithium-7 leaves the 65 pressurized water reactors in the United States vulnerable to supply disruptions. In 2010, for example, we reported on the challenges faced by the Department of Defense when it experienced supply disruptions in rare earth elements—17 elements with unique magnetic properties that are produced almost exclusively in China.[14] Specifically, we reported that a Department of Defense program was delayed due to a shortage of rare earth elements. Controlling most of the market on rare earth materials production, China caused a shortage when it decreased its exports of rare earth materials. At the time of our report, the Department of Defense and other federal agencies were taking steps to mitigate a shortage to prevent future supply disruptions. In the case of lithium-7, according to representatives of two utilities, if not mitigated, a lithium-7 shortage could

---

[14]GAO, *Rare Earth Materials in the Defense Supply Chain*, GAO-10-617R (Washington, D.C.: Apr. 14, 2010).

possibly lead to the shutdown of one or more pressurized water reactors. Pressurized water reactors are temporarily shut down to refuel about every 18 months, after which time lithium-7, in the form of lithium hydroxide, is added to the cooling water, according to industry representatives. TVA representatives explained that nuclear reactors are scheduled for refueling during times when there is low demand for electricity, such as the spring or fall, when there is less need for heating or air-conditioning of homes and businesses. During peak times of electricity use, such as the summer months, commercial nuclear reactors are critical for maintaining the stability of the electrical grid, according to industry representatives. Without lithium hydroxide or some alternative, industry representatives told us that they would not be able to restart the pressurized water reactors after refueling. According to NRC officials, operating a pressurized water reactor without lithium-7 could be done, but it would significantly increase the corrosion of pipes and other infrastructure.

No Entity Has Taken Stewardship Responsibility for Assessing and Managing Risks to the Lithium-7 Supply, but DOE Is Taking Some Actions

No federal entity has taken stewardship responsibility for assessing risks to the lithium-7 supply for the commercial nuclear power industry. However, DOE has taken some steps in this area. Specifically, DOE studied lithium-7 supply and demand and concluded that no further action is needed, but our review found shortcomings in DOE's study.

No Entity Has Taken Stewardship Responsibility for Lithium-7 Risk Assessment

No federal entity has taken stewardship responsibility for assessing and managing risks to the supply of lithium-7 for commercial use. Federal stakeholders—DOE, NRC, and NNSA—told us they view lithium-7 as a commercial commodity for which industry is responsible. Officials in DOE's Isotope Program told us that because lithium-7 is a material bought and sold through commercial channels and used by industry, industry is responsible for monitoring the supply risks and managing those risks as it would do for any other commercial commodity. The Isotope Program produces isotopes that are in short supply and not those that are produced commercially and not in short supply. Notwithstanding, Isotope Program officials told us that the program's mission includes isotopes that have the potential for being in short supply and that they see the Isotope Program's role as being the lead office within DOE on issues related to lithium-7. Additionally, an Isotope Program official told us that the program must be careful not to address lithium-7 risks too aggressively because that may signal to industry stakeholders that DOE is taking responsibility for mitigating these risks—risks that DOE views as the responsibility of industry to manage.

NRC officials also told us that they believe industry is better suited to address any problems with the lithium-7 supply because the utilities are more likely to be aware of and have more information related to supply constraints than NRC or other federal government agencies. Similarly, officials in DOE's Office of Nuclear Energy said that, in their view, industry is responsible for addressing lithium-7 risks, and their office's role is to serve as liaison between DOE and industry. One DOE official said that industry probably would be aware of a shortage before any government agency would be. An official in NNSA's Office of Nuclear Materials Integration noted that NNSA is responsible for ensuring there is a sufficient supply of lithium-7 for federal demand but not for industry's demand. Furthermore, this official said that utilities are in the electricity business and should, therefore, assume the responsibility of assessing and managing risks. This official also stated that, in his view, given the importance of lithium-7 to the nuclear power industry, the commercial market would respond by increasing production to bring supply and demand into balance. However, our review found no other countries with the capability to enrich lithium-7 and, as described above, it is unclear if Russia and China will be able to meet increased demand.

We reported in May 2011 on the importance of stewardship responsibility for critical isotopes. Specifically, our review found that a delayed response to the shortage of helium-3 in 2008 occurred because, among other things, there was no agency with stewardship responsibility to monitor the risks to helium-3 supply and demand.[15] The shortage was addressed when an interagency committee took on a stewardship role by researching alternatives and allocating the limited supply, among other things. In that report, we recommended the Secretary of Energy clarify which entity has a stewardship role for 17 isotopes that are sold by the Isotope Program. In its comments on that report, NNSA stated that it

---

[15]GAO-11-472.

could implement our recommendation, but to date, DOE and NNSA have not determined which entity or entities should serve as steward for lithium-7, and no federal entity has assumed such responsibility.

The nuclear power industry may not be concerned about lithium-7 supply disruptions because it may not be aware of all the risks. Industry representatives we spoke with said that they have no concerns over the lithium-7 supply because they have not experienced any supply problems. For example, representatives from one utility said they have never had a problem obtaining lithium-7 so they did not see a need to consider actions to mitigate future supply disruptions. Similarly, representatives from EPRI said that they are not doing any work related to lithium-7 because there is no demonstrated need. However, EPRI representatives said they were surprised to recently learn from DOE that China is researching the development of molten salt reactors. These representatives said that such a development is important for EPRI's considerations of the lithium-7 issue. EPRI representatives told us they need to learn about all the factors relating to the current and future supply and demand of lithium-7 so those factors can be incorporated into EPRI's decision-making process and long-term planning. We discussed this point with DOE officials, and they were surprised to hear that industry was previously uninformed about China's development of molten salt reactors. An official from DOE's Office of Nuclear Energy told us the risks to the lithium-7 supply had been discussed with industry representatives in October 2012, including China's increased domestic demand for new reactors and for research on molten salt reactors, all of which could impact the lithium-7 supply.

In addition to the longer term supply challenges created by increased Chinese domestic demand for lithium-7, there are also the recent examples of brokers facing supply disruptions. As previously discussed, two of the lithium-7 brokers told us they are having difficulty obtaining lithium-7 from China and Russia. Given the recent nature of this information, the uncertainty over whether these are isolated difficulties or indicative of a trend, and that the impact has not yet been felt by utilities, could also contribute to industry's current assessment that the risks of a possible lithium-7 supply disruption are low. Some industry representatives stated that, if there is a shortage, the federal government should be involved to ensure the reliability of the electrical grid.[16] For example, EPRI representatives said that, in the event of shortage, EPRI's role would be to research options for replacing lithium-7, but also said that government involvement is needed to ensure the reliability of the electrical grid.

Under risk assessment, one of the federal standards for internal control, agencies are to identify and analyze relevant risks, including estimating the risk's significance and likelihood of occurrence, and then decide what actions should be taken to manage the risks.[17] In the case of lithium-7, the steward would, for example, need to ensure risks to the lithium-7 supply are identified, analyzed, communicated to stakeholders, and managed appropriately. The steward would also need to determine and assign proper roles and responsibilities to stakeholders and ensure the completeness and accuracy of data and information for decision making. Such a steward does not necessarily have to be a federal entity or be responsible for all actions; a steward could be an entity from industry, or even a committee of federal and industry stakeholders, each responsible for specific tasks. Another federal standard for internal control states that information should be recorded and communicated to management and others within an entity in a form and within a time frame that enables them to carry out their responsibilities.[18] While these standards may not apply to nonfederal entities, they can provide guidance as to the sorts of internal controls that may be appropriate for stewardship of Lithium-7. Relevant, reliable, and timely communications related to internal, as well as external events, are important for an agency to achieve all its objectives and especially important for managing risks, which involve developing knowledge of the situation to inform decision making on the methods employed to adequately mitigate the risks. In the case of lithium-7, a steward would, for example, need to have adequate information to identify the supply risks and manage them appropriately. Industry does

---

[16]There is a federal agency with responsibility for regulating the reliability of the electrical grid. The Federal Energy Regulatory Commission is an independent agency responsible for the regulation of interstate transmission of electricity, natural gas, and oil. The agency assigns implementation of these activities to the North American Electric Reliability Corporation, a nonprofit entity whose mission is to ensure the reliability of the bu k power system in North America.

[17]GAO/AIMD-00 -21.3.1.

[18] GAO/AIMD-00-21.3.1.

GAO-13-716 Managing Critical Isotopes

not have access to all the sources of information that are available to DOE.

DOE Studied Lithium-7 Supply and Demand and Concluded That No Further Action Is Needed, but Its Study Has Shortcomings

DOE studied the supply and demand of lithium-7 and concluded that no further action is needed to mitigate a potential lithium-7 shortage, but our review found shortcomings in its assessment of domestic demand and the mitigation measures it identifies for industry to consider implementing. In conducting this study, Isotope Program officials collaborated with officials in DOE's Offices of Nuclear Energy and Intelligence and Counterintelligence and NNSA's Office of Nuclear Materials Integration and had discussions with EPRI and other industry representatives.

DOE's study, which was completed in May 2013, identifies some risks to the lithium-7 supply, describes several actions that industry could take to help mitigate a shortage, and lists the steps that DOE's Isotope Program is taking, or plans to take. According to DOE's study, there are several risks to the lithium-7 supply that could result in a shortage in a matter of years. Specifically, DOE's study points out that increasing demand for lithium-7 from construction of additional pressurized water reactors and the development of molten salt reactors are risks to the lithium-7 supply because demand could exceed the supply in a matter of years, if production does not increase. The study also points out the risks of relying on two foreign suppliers for lithium-7 and notes that a supply shortage is a low probability risk, but it is one with high consequence. DOE's study also describes several actions that industry could take to help mitigate a lithium-7 shortage. In its discussions with industry representatives, representatives identified the following four actions that the nuclear power industry could take should a shortage of lithium-7 occur:

- recycling lithium-7 from the demineralizers;

- increasing the burnable poisons in the reactor fuel;[19]

---

[19]Burnable poisons are isotopes in the nuclear fuel that help control the nuclear reaction in the core. Burnable poisons can be added to reactor fuel to provide additional control over the reaction in a reactor core early in its operating cycle, thus reducing the amount of boric acid and lithium hydroxide needed in the cooling water.

- reducing the acidity of the cooling water to reduce the amount of lithium-7 needed by using boric acid that is enriched with boron-10, which would reduce the amount of boric acid added to the cooling water, thus reducing the acidity; and

- developing alternative sources of lithium-7, including building a domestic lithium-7 production capability.

DOE's study of lithium-7 also lists two steps the Isotope Program is taking and concludes that no further action is needed. First, the study states that the Isotope Program will work with NNSA to prevent its inventory of contaminated lithium-7 at Y-12 from being disposed of or distributed without approval from DOE and will request that NNSA retain 200 kilograms (441 pounds) of this inventory to be purified and then sold to the nuclear power industry in the event of a supply disruption.[20] Second, according to Isotope Program officials, as part of its mission to support isotope production research and development, the program is also funding research on enriching lithium-7 without employing the mercury-intensive COLEX method that was previously used. The study concludes that the listed steps serve as an acceptable short-term strategy for mitigating the risks of a lithium-7 shortage and concludes that no additional action is needed.

Nevertheless, our review found several shortcomings in DOE's study regarding its assessment of domestic demand for lithium-7 and the feasibility of the actions it says industry can take to mitigate the risks of a supply disruption. First, our review found that DOE's Isotope Program, as well as Y-12, underestimated domestic demand for lithium-7. While studying lithium-7 supply and demand, DOE's Isotope Program and Y-12 both estimated annual domestic demand for lithium-7 to be about 200 kilograms per year, whereas the lithium-7 brokers estimated domestic demand to be over 300 kilograms (662 pounds) per year, on average, from 2008 through 2012. Isotope Program and Y-12 officials told us that their estimate of 200 kilograms per year includes lithium-7 used in cooling water, but it does not include lithium-7 used in demineralizers, which the

---

[20]The study says that 200 kilograms of the contaminated lithium-7 will be set aside rather than purified now because if a supply disruption occurs, there will be sufficient time to purify it before it is actually needed by the utilities. According to DOE, it will take about 7 months to purify 200 kilograms of lithium-7 and cost about $600,000, which the Isotope Program has agreed to pay for if the reserve is needed.

GAO-13-716 Managing Critical Isotopes

lithium-7 brokers did account for. Second, DOE's study concludes that there is enough lithium-7 in inventory held on-site at reactors to keep the reactors operating during the approximately 7 months required to purify Y-12's lithium-7. However, DOE officials involved in the study said they did not collect any data from utilities to determine what quantities they held in inventory, and industry representatives told us that they are not aware of any entity that keeps records of the amount of lithium-7 inventory held at utilities across the industry. Some industry representatives also said that there is no standard practice for when to purchase lithium-7 or how much inventory to have on hand and that they believe inventory practices vary from utility to utility.

Regarding the measures the study indicates industry can take to mitigate a potential lithium-7 supply shortage, our review found that DOE's study provides more optimistic assessments than industry's view about the challenges involved in implementing these actions. For example, DOE's study characterizes the process for recycling lithium-7 from demineralizers to be straightforward and of low technical risk, and it states that recycling can be implemented within a year. However, according to representatives of a utility with whom we spoke, there is no existing method to retrieve and recycle the lithium-7 from the demineralizers. According to EPRI representatives who provided information for DOE's study, the process is challenging because extracting lithium-7 from the demineralizers may require a special process to separate it from the other materials in the demineralizers, some of which pose radiation risks. In addition, there are also application challenges to recovering the lithium-7, such as modifying the plants to implement the process. EPRI representatives estimated it would take more than a year to develop the technology, and potentially many years to address the application challenges before this process could be implemented. Another mitigation option that DOE's study identifies is increasing burnable poisons—isotopes added to the nuclear fuel to help control the nuclear reaction—that would decrease the amount of boron required in the cooling water, in turn reducing the amount of lithium-7 needed to decrease acidity. The study states that doing so should not take a long time to implement, based on the premise that the modified fuel could be changed when plants refuel, which is about every 18 months. EPRI representatives, however, said this would be a longer process because any given fuel assembly is typically in the reactor for three operating cycles of 18 months each, which means a fuel assembly would be in the reactor for a total of about 4½ years before being replaced. Also, according to NRC officials, a change in the fuel would require extensive modeling, testing, and regulatory reviews, which could take considerably longer than 4½ years. As a result of the shortcomings in DOE's study, combined with the recent supply problems reported by brokers, as we previously discussed, it is unclear if its conclusion is correct that no additional actions need to be taken.

Additional Options Exist to Mitigate a Potential Lithium-7 Shortage

Based on information from government officials and industry representatives, we identified three options for mitigating a potential lithium-7 shortage in the near and long term, which could be implemented by government, industry, or even a committee of federal and industry stakeholders. The three near- and long-term options are: building a domestic reserve of lithium-7, building domestic capability to produce lithium-7, and reducing pressurized water reactors' reliance on lithium-7.

The first option—building a domestic reserve of lithium-7—is a relatively low-cost option and would provide a fixed quantity of lithium-7 that, in the event of a shortage, could be used until a long-term solution is implemented. Establishing a domestic reserve would involve building up a stockpile of lithium-7 by importing an additional quantity above what is needed each year, purifying all or a portion of the existing supply of lithium-7 at Y-12 to make it suitable for use in pressurized water reactors, or a combination of these two. Stockpiling could be accomplished by individual utilities or, for example, by a steward that could maintain the supply for all utilities. Increasing imports to establish a domestic reserve could be initiated immediately, and the cost would be based on the market price of lithium-7, which is currently less than $10,000 per kilogram (about 2.2 lbs). However, stockpiling lithium-7 would have to be carefully managed to avoid a negative impact on the market—stockpiling lithium-7 too aggressively could cause the price to increase or otherwise disrupt the available supply. A second way to help build up a reserve is the purification of all or a portion of the 1,300 kilograms of lithium-7 at Y-12. DOE has plans to set aside 200 kilograms of the 1,300 kilograms of lithium-7 at Y-12, which could be purified and sold to utilities. DOE estimates it would take about 7 months to purify 200 kilograms and cost about $3,000 per kilogram for a total cost of about $600,000; purifying the remainder of the 1,300 kilograms would likely incur additional costs.

The second option—building a domestic lithium-7 production capability—is a longer-term solution that would reduce or eliminate the need for importing supplies, but it would take several years to develop the technology and construct a production facility. While lithium separation was done in the United States until 1963 using the COLEX process, DOE and Y-12 officials told us that the COLEX separation method will not be used for a new production facility because of the large quantities of mercury it requires. Officials from DOE and Y-12, as well as industry representatives, identified several other potential separation techniques that do not use mercury, such as solvent extraction, a process in which the components to be separated are preferentially dissolved by a solvent and are thus separated, and electromagnetic separation, a process that uses electric and magnetic fields to separate isotopes by their relative weights. While these techniques have been developed and used to separate other materials—for example, electromagnetic separation was used to separate isotopes of uranium—further development of the techniques specifically for use with lithium-7 would be needed, according to DOE documentation. In particular, DOE's Isotope Program is funding a proposal from scientists at Oak Ridge National Laboratory and Y-12 to conduct research on lithium separation techniques using solvent extraction processes, which have been used in the pharmaceutical industry. If successful, according to Y-12, its proposed research would provide the basis for an industrial process to produce lithium-7. According to Y-12 officials, the entire research and development process, and the construction of a pilot facility capable of producing 200 kilograms of lithium-7 per year, would take about 5 years and cost $10 to $12 million.

The third option—reducing pressurized water reactors' reliance on lithium-7–is also a longer-term option that would generally require changes in how reactors are operated and may produce only modest reductions in the use of lithium-7. Four possible changes that could be made to reactors include the following:

- Lithium-7 can be recycled from used demineralizers. According to industry representatives, the chemistry required for the recycling process would be challenging, would require plant modifications, and may pose risks to workers due to the presence of radioactive materials. This option would reduce the amount of lithium-7 needed for demineralizers but not reduce the amount of lithium-7 needed for the cooling water.

- Potassium hydroxide can be used in lieu of lithium hydroxide in the cooling water. According to nuclear power industry representatives, making such a change would require about 10 years of research to test the resulting changes in the rate of corrosion of pipes and other infrastructure in the reactor.

- Using enriched boric acid in the cooling water in place of natural boric acid would require less boric acid to be used, which would reduce the acidity of the water and result in less lithium-7 being needed. According to industry representatives, however, enriched boric acid is expensive, and this change may require plant modifications and would only modestly reduce the amount of lithium-7 needed.

- The nuclear fuel used in pressurized water reactors could be modified to reduce the need for boric acid and thus also reduce the amount of lithium-7 needed. According to industry representatives, however, this would be expensive and require long-term planning because utilities typically plan their fuel purchases for refueling 1½ to 4½ years in advance. According to one utility, changing the fuel could also have widespread impacts on operations and costs that are difficult to quantify.

Industry representatives characterized all four possible changes to pressurized water reactors for reducing the demand for lithium-7 as requiring significant modifications to reactor operations at all 65 pressurized water reactors. Furthermore, these possible changes would need to be studied in more detail to determine the associated cost, time, and safety requirements before implementation and, if necessary, approved by NRC, all of which may take several years.

Conclusions

DOE studied the lithium-7 supply and demand situation, including identifying some supply risks, and is undertaking some actions to help mitigate a potential shortage, such as setting aside 200 kilograms of lithium-7 as a reserve. However, relying on two foreign producers to supply a chemical that is critical to the safe operation of most of the commercial nuclear power reactors in the United States places their ability to continue to provide electricity at some risk. Furthermore, the recent problems some brokers reported in obtaining lithium-7 from Russia and China, combined with China's increasing demand for lithium-7 suggest that the potential for a supply problem occurring may be increasing. DOE has not taken on stewardship responsibility, in part because lithium-7 it is not in short supply, at which time it could fall under the Isotope Program's mission. However, waiting for a critical isotope with increasing supply risks to become short in supply before taking action does not appear consistent with the mission of the Isotope Program. Because no entity has assumed stewardship responsibility for lithium-7, supply risks may not have been effectively communicated to industry, which could then weigh the risks and respond appropriately. Furthermore, there is no assurance that the risks have been fully analyzed and mitigated, as outlined in federal standards for internal control. Similarly, a shortage of helium-3 occurred in 2008 because, among other things, there was no agency with stewardship responsibility to monitor the risks to helium-3 supply and demand. The shortage was addressed when an interagency committee took on a stewardship role by researching alternatives and allocating the limited supply, among other things. Some DOE officials have described lithium-7 as a commercial commodity used by industry and, therefore, they assert that industry is responsible for addressing any supply problems, despite its importance to the electrical grid; NNSA and NRC concur that industry is responsible. Yet, industry is not in a position like DOE to be aware of all the risks. DOE has studied lithium-7 supply and demand to guide its decisions related to lithium-7. However, its study contains shortcomings, including underestimating the domestic demand, and may be underestimating the technological challenges industry will face in trying to adjust to a supply disruption. These shortcomings bring into question DOE's conclusion that no additional actions are needed to mitigate a potential lithium-7 shortage. In the end, without a full awareness of supply risks and an accurate assessment of domestic demand, utilities may not be prepared for a shortage of lithium-7. This leaves the reactors that depend on lithium-7 vulnerable to supply disruptions that, if not addressed, could lead to their shutdown.

Recommendation for Executive Action

To ensure a stable future supply of lithium-7, we recommend that the Secretary of Energy direct the Isotope Program, consistent with the program's mission to manage isotopes in short supply, to take on the stewardship role by fully assessing supply risks; communicating risks, as needed, to stakeholders; ensuring risks are appropriately managed; and fully and accurately determining domestic demand.

Agency Comments and Our Evaluation

We provided a draft of this report to DOE and NRC for review and comment. In written comments, DOE's Office of Science's Acting Director, responding on behalf of DOE, wrote that DOE concurred with our recommendation. DOE's written comments on our draft report are included in appendix I. In an e-mail received August 15, 2013, NRC's Audit Liaison in the Office of the Executive Director for Operations stated that NRC generally agreed with the report's content and recommendation. DOE and NRC provided technical comments that we incorporated as appropriate.

In its comment letter, DOE concurred with our recommendation and stated that, in its view, ongoing efforts by DOE's Isotope Program satisfy the recommendation. Specifically, DOE's letter states that to further address lithium-7 utilization, demand, and inventory management, the Isotope Program has initiated the development of a more in-depth survey coordinated directly with the power industry through the Electric Power Research Institute—a new undertaking that we learned about after providing a draft of our report to DOE for comment. We believe that this undertaking is especially important since we found that few people in industry were aware of the lithium-7 supply risks.

In its written comments, DOE also states that the report includes several inaccurate descriptions of the federal role with respect to the response to lithium-7 availability and demand. Specifically, DOE does not agree with our characterization that there is a lack of federal stewardship for assessing and managing risks to the lithium-7 supply. DOE states that it has been active in assessing and managing supply risks, including engaging with stakeholders, forming an internal working group, and identifying actions to be taken to mitigate a shortage.

We disagree and believe that DOE's comment letter overstates both the department's level of awareness of lithium-7 supply risks and its involvement in mitigating these risks. At no time during our review did any DOE official characterize DOE as a steward of lithium-7 or state that the agency will manage supply risks. Notably, during our review, the Director of the Facilities and Project Management Division, who manages the Isotope Program, told us that the Isotope Program is not the steward of lithium-7, nor should it be. Regarding engagement with stakeholders, we found that Isotope Program officials were aware of only two of the three key brokers of lithium-7 until we informed them of the third broker during a meeting in June 2013—over a year after the program became aware of a potential lithium-7 supply problem. Moreover, at this same meeting, program officials were not yet aware of recent lithium-7 supply problems experienced by two of the three lithium-7 brokers. Regarding mitigation actions, while DOE states in its comment letter that industry stakeholders identified actions for consideration should a shortage of lithium-7 occur, industry stakeholders told us that they were not aware that their input was being used for a DOE study and would not characterize the actions as DOE did in its study.

We also disagree with DOE's comment letter suggesting that the shortcomings identified in our report regarding the department's demand estimates for lithium-7 were simply due to differences between our

GAO-13-716 Managing Critical Isotopes

estimates and the DOE internal working group's estimates as a result of the demand quantities identified being for specific and different applications. To identify the actions needed to mitigate a lithium-7 shortage, all the uses of lithium-7 must be considered. By not accounting for the lithium-7 used in demineralizers, DOE left out an important use of lithium-7 that may represent about one-third of the total demand for pressurized water reactors. As DOE engages collaboratively with industry for ensuring a stable supply of lithium-7, accurately accounting for lithium-7 demand will be essential.

As agreed with your office, unless you publicly announce the contents of this report earlier, we plan no further distribution until 30 days from the report date. At that time, we will send copies to the appropriate congressional committees, Secretary of Energy, Executive Director for Operations of NRC, and other interested parties. In addition, the report will be available at no charge on the GAO website at http://www.gao.gov.

If you or your staff members have any questions about this report, please contact David C. Trimble at (202) 512-3841 or trimbled@gao.gov or Dr. Timothy M. Persons at (202) 512-6412 or personst@gao.gov. Contact points for our Offices of Congressional Relations and Public Affairs may be found on the last page of this report. GAO staff who made key contributions to this report are listed in appendix II.

Sincerely yours,

David C. Trimble
Director, Natural Resources and Environment

Timothy M. Persons, Ph.D., Chief Scientist
Director, Center for Science, Technology, and Engineering

Appendix I: Comments from the Department of Energy

Department of Energy
Office of Science
Washington, DC 20585

September 9, 2013

Mr. David Trimble
Director, Natural Resources and Environment
Government Accountability Office
441 G Street
Washington, D.C. 20548

Dear Mr. Trimble,

Thank you for the opportunity to comment on the draft Government Accountability Office (GAO) report entitled, "Managing Critical Isotopes: Stewardship of Lithium-7 is Needed to Ensure a Stable Supply" (GAO-13-716). We have reviewed the draft report and provide these comments (technical comments attached). The comments provided here have been coordinated with appropriate offices within the Department of Energy (DOE). The Office of Science is providing this response for the Department.

We understand that the Energy and Environment and the Investigations and Oversight Subcommittees of the House Committee on Science, Space, and Technology requested that GAO "...(1) assess the known supply and domestic demand for lithium-7; (2) determine the roles of DOE and other departments or agencies in monitoring the availability of lithium-7 and what actions have been taken to date to address any future shortages; and (3) identify options that may exist for producing lithium-7 domestically and what alternative materials are available to replace lithium-7." DOE has been actively engaged in the topic of lithium-7 availability and appreciates the Committee's attention to this important topic.

The DOE Isotope Program is managed by the Office of Nuclear Physics (NP) within the Office of Science. The Program has the mission to produce and distribute high priority stable isotopes and radioisotopes that are in short supply for research and applications, and to support research aimed at improving or developing production techniques for high priority isotopes that are in short supply. In order to implement this mission effectively, the Isotope Program works closely with federal agencies, academia, and commercial stakeholders to understand general isotope demand and priorities and potential risks to supply chains. Over the past four years, NP has implemented significant improvements to strengthen the DOE Isotope Program, including strengthened communication with stakeholders, development of new production techniques, and increased availability of high priority isotopes.

The DOE Isotope Program became aware of potential risks in the commercial supply of lithium-7 in January of 2012, and accordingly, established an internal DOE working group to investigate this topic with participating members from the National Nuclear Security Administration, Office of Intelligence, and Office of Nuclear Energy. This group has worked effectively with federal and industrial stakeholders, including representatives from the nuclear power industry, to assess aspects of lithium-7 supply and demand and to develop a suite of actions to mitigate risks in the availability of this commercial isotope; these actions were shared with GAO during the audit.

Printed with soy ink on recycled paper

The Department finds the draft GAO report to include several inaccurate descriptions of the federal role with respect to the response to lithium-7 availability and demand. DOE does not agree with GAO's characterization that there is a lack of federal stewardship for assessing and managing risks to the lithium-7 supply. While it is not reasonable or appropriate for the U.S. government to accept stewardship responsibilities for all isotopes, particularly those that are commercially available, DOE does recognize the need to assess risks to supply chains of critical isotopes and to understand demand for certain isotopes so as to predict, mitigate, and react to potential shortages. DOE has been active in assessing and managing the risks to lithium-7 supplies, including engaging with stakeholders, forming an internal DOE working group on lithium-7, and identifying actions to be taken to mitigate a potential shortage.

The draft report inaccurately states that, following its study by the internal working group, DOE had concluded that no further action is needed with respect to a potential lithium-7 shortage. This is not correct. DOE first pointed out this inaccuracy when it reviewed the GAO's initial Statement of Facts. It is disappointing that the GAO chose to not recognize in the draft report the actions that the DOE identified and that are actively being implemented to mitigate a potential shortage of lithium-7. These actions include: (1) the creation of a substantial lithium-7 inventory; (2) the positioning of a capability to process lithium-7 in a timely manner; (3) the support of R&D to develop new lithium-7 production techniques; (4) the collaborative efforts with industry to demonstrate the feasibility of lithium-7 recycling; (5) the collaborative efforts with industry to improve the management of their own inventory of lithium-7; and (6) the continued monitoring of the lithium-7 supply chain.

The draft report suggests there are "shortcomings" in the DOE assessment of domestic demand of lithium-7 and in the feasibility of the actions that industry can take to mitigate a supply shortage of lithium-7. DOE acknowledges that the demand estimates by GAO, based on their interviews with industry and brokers, and the estimates by DOE internal working group are different. However, the difference results from the fact that the demand quantities identified were for specific and different applications. Further, in regard to GAO's remarks on the feasibility of the actions that industry can take to mitigate a shortage, it should be understood and noted that the actions identified and provided in the internal working group study were not developed by DOE, but represent a summary of actions identified by industry stakeholders themselves for consideration should a shortage occur. DOE will continue to engage with industry collaboratively on this matter, and has already initiated the development of a more in depth survey in cooperation with the Electric Power Research Institute to clarify utilization, demand, inventory management, and approach to lithium-7 purchase.

DOE remains committed to working with federal, academic, and industrial stakeholders in increasing the availability of high priority isotopes that are in short supply and mitigating potential shortages of isotopes. If you have any questions on this matter please feel free to contact Dr. Jehanne Gillo at (301) 903-1455.

Sincerely,

Patricia M. Dehmer
Acting Director, Office of Science

Attachment

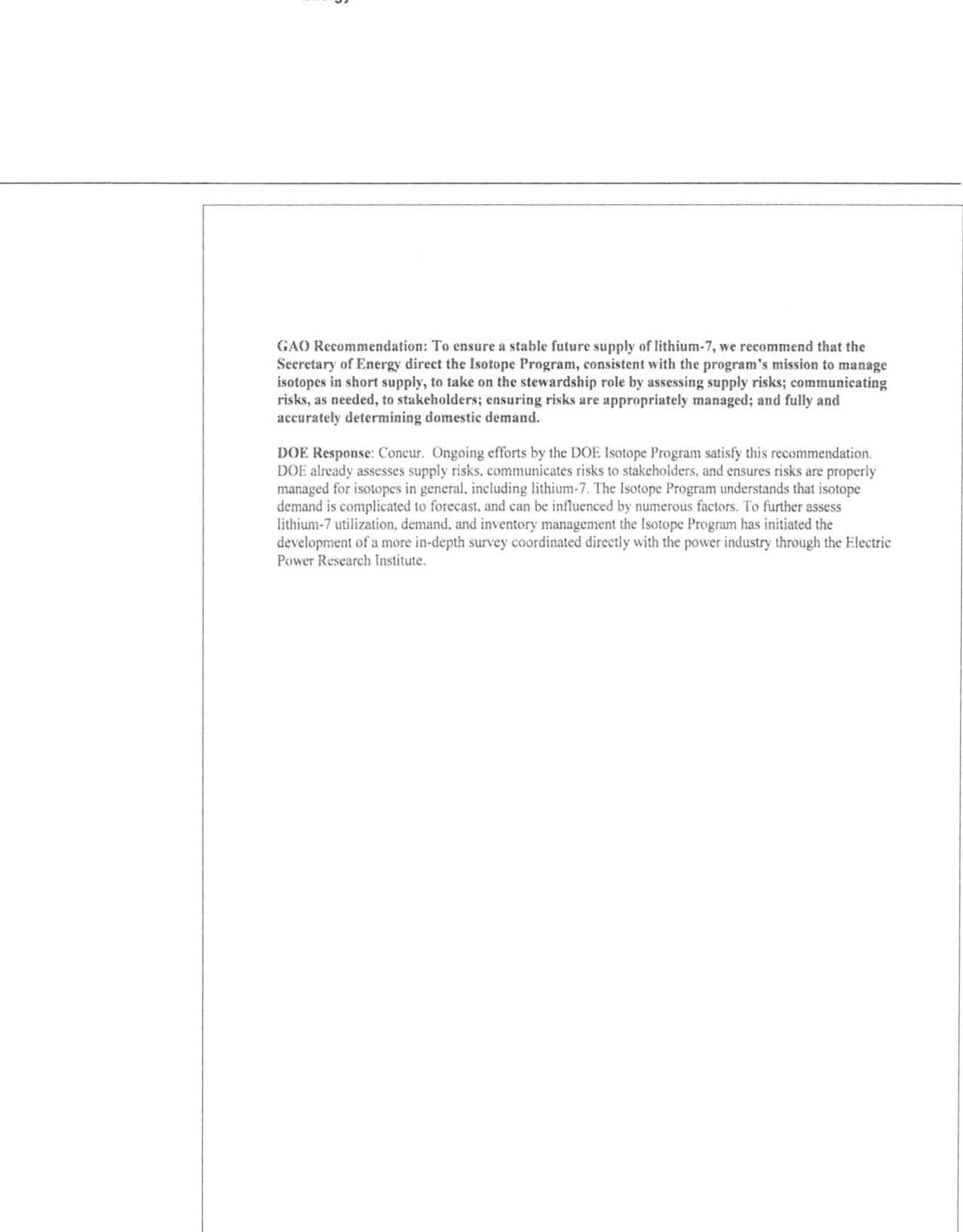

GAO Recommendation: To ensure a stable future supply of lithium-7, we recommend that the
Secretary of Energy direct the Isotope Program, consistent with the program's mission to manage
isotopes in short supply, to take on the stewardship role by assessing supply risks; communicating
risks, as needed, to stakeholders; ensuring risks are appropriately managed; and fully and
accurately determining domestic demand.

DOE Response: Concur. Ongoing efforts by the DOE Isotope Program satisfy this recommendation.
DOE already assesses supply risks, communicates risks to stakeholders, and ensures risks are properly
managed for isotopes in general, including lithium. The Isotope Program understands that isotope
demand is complicated to forecast, and can be influenced by numerous factors. To further assess
lithium-7 utilization, demand, and inventory management the Isotope Program has initiated the
development of a more in-depth survey coordinated directly with the power industry through the Electric
Power Research Institute.

Appendix II: GAO Contacts and Staff Acknowledgments

GAO Contacts	David C. Trimble, (202) 512-3841 or trimbled@gao.gov Dr. Timothy M. Persons, (202) 512-6412 or personst@gao.gov
Staff Acknowledgments	In addition to the individuals named above, Ned H. Woodward, Assistant Director; R. Scott Fletcher; Wyatt R. Hundrup; and Franklyn Yao made key contributions to this report. Kevin Bray, Cindy Gilbert, Karen Howard, Mehrzad Nadji, and Alison O'Neill also made important contributions.

www.ingramcontent.com/pod-product-compliance
Lightning Source LLC
Chambersburg PA
CBHW080752290526
45790CB00008B/3425